THAT'S NOT THE PEAK --
YOU'RE STANDING ON A MOGUL

**SALAD BAR IS NOT THE
NAME OF A SKI RUN**

SKI SIGNALS
For Beginners

by Graham Harrop

ISBN-13: 978-1541023710

**GOOD NEWS. YOUR DOCTOR IS
THE ONE YOU RAN INTO**

**YOUR SKIS DOUBLE
AS CRUTCHES**

**THE RED CROSS HAS VOTED
YOU DONOR OF THE YEAR**

WHERE DO YOU WANT YOUR EQUIPMENT SENT?

**FLAP YOUR ARMS -- YOU'VE
JUST SKIED OVER A CLIFF**

YOU JUST WIPED OUT THE ENTIRE
HAPPY VALLEY SKI SCHOOL

WE FOUND YOUR OTHER EAR

**YOU HAVEN'T LOST YOUR TIPS --
YOUR SKIS ARE ON BACKWARDS**

**WE HAVE NO IDEA WHERE
THE COW CAME FROM**

**THE SKI PATROL IS GOING TO
NAME THE MOUNTAIN AFTER YOU**

YOU'LL BE ON THE 11:00 NEWS

**THAT'S NOT A ST. BERNARD
YOU'RE PETTING**

**THE LODGE IS BILLING YOU
FOR THEIR DOORS**

**YOUR LAST RUN QUALIFIES
FOR FEDERAL AID**

CHAIRLIFTS ARE JUST ONE WAY

**THAT WAS HULK HOGAN
YOU JUST KNOCKED OVER**

YOU CAN'T USE YOUR POLES AS TURN SIGNALS

**DON'T WORRY -- THEY CAN USE
THE TREE FOR FIREWOOD**

**THE SKI SCHOOL IS GIVING
YOU YOUR MONEY BACK**

**YOU'RE NOT BLEEDING --
YOUR WINESKIN BROKE**

LET THE BEAR HAVE YOUR SKIS

Printed in Great Britain
by Amazon